Pocket

FIRST LADIES

Wisdom

Pocket

FIRST LADIES

Wisdom

**Wise words and inspirational
ideas from America's first ladies**

Hardie Grant

B O O K S

CONTENTS

INTRODUCTION

★

Imagine taking on a job that involves you being publicly scrutinized—from the way you wear your hair, to how you dress and the loyalty you hold for your country—and not being paid one single cent. Welcome to the job of being America's First Lady, which Pat Nixon famously described as "the hardest unpaid job in the world"! Next to each US President has stood a First Lady, many of whom were strong-willed, intelligent and hardworking, and who also changed the course of history. They organized state dinners, shaped national conversations, traveled the world—and had to give up their own jobs while their husbands have been in office. This is a celebration of these amazing women and includes their best quotes and advice.

ON
BEING
FIRST LADY

"I don't feel that because I'm First Lady, I'm very different from what I was before. It can happen to anyone. After all, it has happened to anyone."

BETTY FORD

"The First Lady role is really difficult. It has no job description... You have to create it for yourself."

HILLARY CLINTON

"For eight years, I was sleeping with the president, and if that doesn't give you special access, I don't know what does!"

NANCY REAGAN

"I'll be a wife and mother first,
then First Lady."

JACKIE KENNEDY

"No news at 4:30 a.m. is good."

CLAUDIA "LADY BIRD" JOHNSON

"Being first lady is the hardest unpaid job in the world."

PAT NIXON

"If I want to knock a story off the front page, I just change my hairstyle."

HILLARY CLINTON

"The one thing I do not want to be called is First Lady. It sounds like a saddle horse."

JACKIE KENNEDY

ON
BEING
A
WOMAN

"I am a woman above
everything else."

JACKIE KENNEDY

"We need to do a better job of putting ourselves higher on our own 'to-do' list."

MICHELLE OBAMA

"I have an independent streak.
You know, it's kind of hard to
tell an independent woman
what to do."

BETTY FORD

"If particular care and attention is not paid to the ladies, we are determined to foment a rebellion, and will not hold ourselves bound by any laws in which we have no voice, or representation."

ABIGAIL ADAMS

"Every woman over fifty should stay in bed until noon."

MAMIE EISENHOWER

"There is no formula that I'm aware of for being a successful or fulfilled woman today."

HILLARY CLINTON

"The independent girl is truly quite of modern origin, and usually is a most bewitching little piece of humanity."

LOU HENRY HOOVER

"What is sad for women of my generation is that they weren't supposed to work if they had families. What were they going to do when the children are grown—watch the raindrops coming down the window pane?"

JACKIE KENNEDY

"A woman is like a teabag: you cannot tell how strong she is until you put her in hot water."

ELEANOR ROOSEVELT

"Being a lady does not
require silence."

BETTY FORD

ON
SUCCESS

"Success is only meaningful
and enjoyable if it feels like
your own."

MICHELLE OBAMA

"If you don't accept failure as a possibility, you don't set high goals, you don't branch out, you don't try—you don't take the risk."

ROSALYNN CARTER

"Believe in something larger
than yourself... get involved
in the big ideas of your time."

BARBARA BUSH

"You should never view your challenges as a disadvantage. Instead, it's important for you to understand that your experience facing and overcoming adversity is actually one of your biggest advantages."

MICHELLE OBAMA

"You have to have confidence in your ability and then be tough enough to follow through."

ROSALYNN CARTER

"Never lose sight of the fact that the most important yardstick of your success will be how you treat other people—your family, friends, and co-workers, and even strangers you meet along the way."

BARBARA BUSH

ON
EDUCATION

"Education is the single-most important civil rights issue that we face today."

MICHELLE OBAMA

"Learning is not attained by chance; it must be sought for with ardour and diligence."

ABIGAIL ADAMS

"The clash of ideas is the sound of freedom."

CLAUDIA "LADY BIRD" JOHNSON

"While one can lose oneself
in a book one can never be
thoroughly unhappy."

EDITH ROOSEVELT

"I deplore any action which denies artistic talent an opportunity to express itself because of prejudice against race origin."

BESS TRUMAN

"The power of a book lies in its power to turn a solitary act into a shared vision. As long as we have books, we are not alone."

LAURA BUSH

ON
ACTIVISM

"We should all do something to right the wrongs that we see and not just complain about them."

JACKIE KENNEDY

"We have too many high-sounding words, and too few actions that correspond with them."

ABIGAIL ADAMS

"Voting is the most precious right of every citizen, and we have a moral obligation to ensure the integrity of our voting process."

HILLARY CLINTON

"We must choose between a world of fear and a world of progress. We cannot stand by and do nothing while dangers gather."

LAURA BUSH

"Doing the impossible is the history of this nation. It is how this country was built."

MICHELLE OBAMA

"That's what we're here on this Earth for, to help others."

BETTY FORD

ON
FEMINISM

"Human rights are women's rights, and women's rights are human rights."

HILLARY CLINTON

"The search for human freedom
can never be complete without
freedom for women."

BETTY FORD

"I don't think feminism, as
I understand the definition,
implies the rejection of maternal
values, nurturing children,
caring about the men in your life.
That is just nonsense to me."

HILLARY CLINTON

"No country can ever truly flourish if it stifles the potential of its women and deprives itself of the contributions of half its citizens."

MICHELLE OBAMA

"Feminism is the ability to choose what you want to do."

NANCY REAGAN

"Our global future depends on
the willingness of every nation
to invest in its people, especially
women and children."

HILLARY CLINTON

ON
LIFE

"Do what you feel in your heart
to be right—for you'll be
criticized anyway."

ELEANOR ROOSEVELT

"You don't just luck into things as much as you'd like to think you do. You build by step, whether it's friendships or opportunities."

BARBARA BUSH

"The way you overcome shyness
is to become so wrapped up
in something that you forget
to be afraid."

CLAUDIA "LADY BIRD" JOHNSON

"To handle yourself, use your head; to handle others, use your heart."

ELEANOR ROOSEVELT

"I feel like every day,
every minute I have
to make the most of."

HILLARY CLINTON

"You learn something out of everything, and you come to realize more than ever that we're all here for a certain space of time, and then it's going to be over, and you better make this count."

NANCY REAGAN

"I am fond of only what comes
from the heart."

MARTHA WASHINGTON

"It is wonderful to be in on the creation of something, see it used, and then walk away and smile at it."

CLAUDIA "LADY BIRD" JOHNSON

"Helping another person gives
one the deepest pleasure in
the world."

PAT NIXON

"No one can make you feel
inferior without your consent."

ELEANOR ROOSEVELT

"Choose people
who lift you up."

MICHELLE OBAMA

"A little stress and adventure is good for you, if nothing else, just to prove you are alive."

CLAUDIA "LADY BIRD" JOHNSON

ON
POTUS

"I know what's best for the President. I put him in the White House. He does well when he listens to me and poorly when does not."

FLORENCE HARDING

"People don't understand that all presidents, the minute they become president, get a knock at the door. And there's a man there saying, 'Let's talk about your funeral.' At the time I thought, God, that's a terrible thing. Later on, I thought it was pretty wise."

NANCY REAGAN

"One thing I can say about George... he may not be able to keep a job, but he's not boring."

BARBARA BUSH

"A leader takes people where they want to go. A great leader takes people where they don't necessarily want to go, but ought to be."

ROSALYNN CARTER

"I've seen first-hand that being president doesn't change who you are. It reveals who you are."

MICHELLE OBAMA

"Every woman is entitled to an opinion, and the right to express that opinion—especially to the man she's married to."

NANCY REAGAN

ON
HOPE

"The greater part of our happiness or misery depends on our dispositions and not our circumstances."

MARTHA WASHINGTON

"If human beings are perceived as potentials rather than problems, as possessing strengths instead of weaknesses, as unlimited rather than dull and unresponsive, then they thrive and grow to their capabilities."

BARBARA BUSH

"Tomorrow is a mystery.
Today is a gift. That is why
it is called the present."

ELEANOR ROOSEVELT

"Where flowers bloom,
so does hope."

CLAUDIA "LADY BIRD" JOHNSON

"There's a big, wonderful world out there for you. It belongs to you. It's exciting and stimulating and rewarding. Don't cheat yourselves out of this promise."

NANCY REAGAN

"I think that if you live long enough, you realize that so much of what happens in your life is out of your control, but how you respond to it is in your control. That's what I try to remember."

HILLARY CLINTON

SOURCES

Allen, E. 2016. 'Remember the Ladies.' Library of Congress Blog (online) Available at: https://blogs.loc.gov/loc/2016/03/remember-the-ladies/ – p. 23

Ambrose, S. 1990. *Eisenhower Soldier and President: The Renowned One – Volume Life*. Simon & Schuster Paperbacks: New York – p. 24

Angier, M. and Pond, M. 2005. *101 Best Ways to Get Ahead*. USA: Success Networks International, Inc. – p. 34.

Berger, S. 2015. 'Nancy Reagan, Second GOP Debate Host: 10 Quotes from the Former First Lady About Politics and Life in the White House.' *Ibtimes* [online] [Accessed: 2 March 2020] Available from: http://ibtimes.com/ – p. 83

Bouchier, D. 2019. *Dark Matters: Delusions, Illusions, Lost Causes and Absurdities in Modern America*. USA: Lulu Publishing Services – p. 52

Boyack, C. 2012. *Latter-Day Responsibility: Choosing Liberty Through Personal Accountability*. USA: Cedar Fort, Inc. – p. 51

Broach, J. 2015. *Politicians Without Borders: How the Far Right and the Far Left Keep Screwing it Up for All of Us in the Far Centre*. USA: Author House – p. 82

Busch, M. 2017. '11 Famous first Lady Quotes, Side-By-Side With Melania Trump's'. Bustle Online. Available at: https://www.bustle.com/p/11-famous-first-lady-quotes-side-by-side-with-melania-trumps-2742365 – pp. 21, 22

Bush, L. 2010. *Spoken from the Heart*. USA: Scribner – p. 53

Butler, W. 2011. *It's Always Today*. USA: Hollawood Publishing – p. 92

Chhatwal, G. 2018. *Triumphant Thirty! Tap into the Unstoppable to do the Impossible*. Chennai: Notion Press – p. 35

Chozick, A. 2015. 'Hillary Clinton's Beijing Speech on Women Resonates 20 Years Later.' *NY Times* [online] Available at: http://nytimes.com/ – p. 58

Cummings, C. 2019. *The Bold Maneuver: The Ambitious Woman's Playbook for Achieving Greater Success*. USA: Moran James – p. 66

Demakis, J. 2012. *The Ultimate Book of Quotations*. Raleigh, N.C.: Lulu Enterprises – pp. 27, 87

Demetrakis, C. *Faith to Conquer Fear: Inspiration to Achieve Your Dreams*. USA: iUniverse – p. 33

Desmond, K. 2008. *Planet Savers: 301 extraordinary Environmentalists*. New York: Greenleaf Publishing Limited – p. 44

Estrada, S. 2015. 'Michelle Obama: Education is Today's Important Civil-Rights Issue'. *Diversity Inc*. Available at: https://www.diversityinc.com/michelle-obama-education-todays-important-civil-rights-issue/ – p. 40

Fernandez, C. 2016. '26 Michelle Obama Quotes that will Inspire You to Live Your Best Life.' *The Oprah Magazine*. Available at: https://www.oprahmag.com/life/relationships-love/g25438427/michelle-obama-quotes/ – p. 32

Flaherty, T. 2004. *What Jackier Taught us: Lessons from the Remarkable Life of Jacqueline Kennedy Onassis*. USA: Penguin – p. 13

Friedman, K. 2010. *Shut Up and Say Something: Business Communication Strategies to Overcome Challenges and Influence Listeners*. USA: ABC-CLIO, LLC – p. 69

Friedman, L. 2016. *A Twist of Fate*. USA: Darby Creek – p. 78

Gallo, C. 2014. 'The Evolution of the First Lady.' *Her Campus*. Available at: https://www.hercampus.com/school/american/evolution-first-lady – p. 11

Gard, M. & Pluim, C. 2014. 'Schools and Public Health: Past, Present, Future.' USA: Lexington Books – p. 94

Goldin, K. 2018. 'Great Leaders Take People Where They May Not Want to Go.' *Forbes* [online] [Accessed: March 2020] Available at: http://forbes.com/ – p. 85

Goodwin, D. 2013. *The Bully Pulpit*. New York: Simon & Schuster Paperbacks – p. 45

Gourley, C. 2008. *Ms. And the Material Girls: Perceptions of Women from the 1970's through the 1990's*. USA: Twenty-First Century Books

Grimes, A. 1990. *Running Mates: The Making of a First Lady*. USA: William Morrow & Co – p. 67

Grizzard, F. 2002. *George Washington: A Biographical Companion*. USA: ABC-CLIO, inc – p. 90

Harwood, E. 2017. 'Hillary Clinton Debuted New Bangs at Her International Woman's Day Speech.' *Vanity Fair* [online] Available at: https://www.vanityfair.com/style/2017/03/hillary-clinton-international-womens-day-speech – p. 16

Hechkoff, S. 2019. 'Words to Live By: Jacqueline Kennedy Onassis on Womanhood, Power, and Life.' *CR Fashion Book*. Available at: www.crfashionbook.com – p. 20

Hirsch, S. 2015. *Thresholds: How to Thrive Through Life's Transitions to Live*

Fearlessly and Regret Free. USA: Crown Publishing – p. 95

Howe, S. 2016. *'Remember the First Lades.'* New America Org (online) Available at: https://www.newamerica.org/weekly/edition-126/remember-first-ladies/ – p. 15

Johnson, C. 1970. *A White House Diary.* USA: University of Texas Press – pp. 14, 79, 93

Keller, M. 2017. 'A First Lady with Authentic Leadership.' [online] [Accessed: 2 March 2020] Available from: http://sites.psu.edu/ – p. 55

Kukolic, S. 2017. *The Treasure You Seek: A Year's Reflection on Inspiration and Change.* Canada: Friesen Press – p. 73

Lindsay, J. 2018. 'Barbara Bush Quotes to Remember After the Former First Lady's Death at 92.' Metro [online] [Accessed: 2 Mach 2020] Available from: http://metro.co.uk – p. 91

Lord, D. 2018. 'Barbara Bush in her Own Words: Quotes from the Former First Lady.' *Atlanta News Now* [online] [Accessed: 2 March 2020] Available from: http://ajc.com/ – p. 84

Louv, R. 2013. 'The Rarest of Causes: Connecting with Nature Brings us Together.' [online] [Accessed: 2 March 2020]. Available at: http://childrenandnature.org/ – p. 43

Marschhausen, J. 2017. *'Life in Focus: Living and Leading for Educators and Learners.'* [online] [Accessed: 2 March 2020]. Available from: www.lifeinfocus.me

Marshall, J. 2015. *Wda Adjudication manual and Rule Book.* USA: Lulu Publishing Services – p. 75

Mayne. B. 2009. *Self Mapping: How to Awaken to Your True Self.* Great Britain: Watkins Publishing – p. 71

McCubbin, L. 2018. *Betty Ford: First Lady, Women's Advocate, Survivor, Trailblazer.* USA: Gallery Books – p. 59

Moore, M. & Moore, R. (ed) 2001. *New Meanings for Marketing in a New Millennium.* California: Springer Cham – p. 36

Nagel, P. 1987. *The Adams Women: Abigail and Louisa Adams, Their Sisters and Daughters.* USA: Harvard University Press – p. 70

Obama, M. 2012. *Democratic National Convention Speech.* 4 September, National Convention Centre, Charlotte, NC.

Obama, M. 2012. *Remarks by the First Lady at the Democratic National Convention.* 5 September, Time Warner Cable Arena, Charlotte, North Carolina – p. 86

Obama, M. 2014. *Remarks by the First Lady at the Summit of the Mandela Washington Fellowship for Young African Leaders*. 30 July, The Omni Shoreham Hotel, Washington DC. – p. 61

Phillips, M. 2013. *The Tiniest God*. USA: Lulu Publishing Services – p. 63

Prys, M. & Macgregor, J. 2013. *Faith of the First Ladies*. United Kingdom: Baker Books – p. 76

Roberts, W. 2002. *The Best Advice Ever for Leaders*. USA: New Word City Publishers – p. 37

Swanson, J. 2013. '"*The President has been Shot!*": The Assassination of John F. Kennedy.' Scholastic Inc – p. 50

Theobald. J. 2016. *What the Raven Brings*. United Kingdom: Head of Zeus – p. 28

Tobin, L. 1990. 'Betty Ford as First Lady.' Presidential Studies Quarterly. 20. p. 764 – p. 29

Tumulty, K. 97 'Hillary Rodham Clinton: Turning Fifty.' *All Politics CNN*. Available at: https://edition.cnn.com/ALLPOLITICS/1997/10/13/time/hillary.html – p. 25

Waldrop, M. and Miller, J. (ed) 2014. *Wit and Wisdom of America's First Ladies: A Book of Quotations.*' Dover publications, USA – pp. 10, 12, 17, 74

Watson, R. and Eksterowicz, A. (ed). 2006 *The Presidential Companion: Readings on the First Ladies*. USA: The University of South Carolina Press – p. 62

Weekes, K. 2007. *Women Know Everything!: 241 Quips, Quotes & Brilliant Remarks*. USA: Quirk Books – p. 68

Wertheimer, M. ed. 2004. *Inventing a Voice: The Rhetoric of American First Ladies of the Twentieth Century*. USA: Rowman & Littlefield Publishers – pp. 46, 47

Williams, J. 2003. *We Guarantee Academic Success! Reflections*. USA: iUniverse – p. 77

Wong, P. 2009. *Martyrs in Paradise*. Author House: Indiana – p. 26

Published in 2020 by Hardie Grant Books,
an imprint of Hardie Grant Publishing

Hardie Grant Books (London)
5th & 6th Floors
52–54 Southwark Street
London SE1 1UN

Hardie Grant Books (Melbourne)
Building 1, 658 Church Street
Richmond, Victoria 3121

hardiegrantbooks.com

British Library Cataloguing-in-Publication Data. A catalogue
record for this book is available from the British Library.

Pocket First Ladies Wisdom
ISBN: 978-1-78488-380-5

10 9 8 7 6 5 4 3 2 1

Publishing Director: Kate Pollard
Editorial Assistant: Alexandra Lidgerwood
Design and Art Direction: Studio Noel

Colour reproduction by p2d
Printed and bound in China by Leo Paper Products Ltd.

MIX
Paper from
responsible sources
FSC® C020056
FSC
www.fsc.org